How to Make birthday and Christmas cards

How to

Make birthday and Christmas cards

Andrew Withers

STUDIO VISTA London

 VAN NOSTRAND REINHOLD COMPANY New York

SEP 10 1974

A Studio Vista/Van Nostrand Reinhold How-to Book

Photoset, printed and bound in England by
BAS Printers Limited, Wallop, Hampshire

Published in Great Britain by
Studio Vista
Blue Star House, Highgate Hill, London N19
and in the United States by
Van Nostrand Reinhold Company
A Division of Litton Educational Publishing, Inc.
450 West 33rd Street, New York, N.Y. 10001.

Library of Congress Catalog Card Number 72–39847

ISBN 0 289 70256 9

Contents

Introduction

Have you ever noticed that friends and relations are always extra pleased with presents that you have made yourself? The same is true of birthday and Christmas cards, for a hand-made card will give much more pleasure than any bought in a shop.

This book gives instructions for making many different kinds of cards; but it is up to you to find just the right design for them. Try to fit each card as closely as possible either to the occasion or to the person for whom it is intended. You could use that person's birth sign or favourite colour, or perhaps he or she is fond of animals, or has a hobby that will suggest a suitable design. In this way you will make each card truly unique.

And you need not stop at birthdays and Christmas. Why not adapt some of these ideas to make Easter cards, anniversary cards, good luck cards, get well cards, and so on. Page 67 will help you to think up cards to fit almost any occasion, and you will have a great deal of fun making them.

Decoration

Some of the more attractive cards you see in the shops are purely decorative and rely for effect on a colourful pattern or a message in gay lettering. It is the decoration which makes the card individual and personal. Decoration adds interest to your greeting by enlivening it with colour or enriching it with pattern.

7

Any simple shape can be a starting point for a design. You can add to it, repeat it, alter it, or use it with other shapes. Some designs are built up using one shape only. Others make use of several different shapes.

Look at the shapes on this page. Copy them. Invent new ones. Develop some of the shapes by adding more decoration. Notice how different they look when you draw them large or small or when you use pencils, crayons or paints.

Try to think what makes something decorative.

If you take a photograph of a cat, you will be making a life-like copy of it. It may look very appealing, but it will not be decorative. The drawing of the cat on this page, on the other hand, does not look very life-like, but it is both pretty and decorative.

Nature will give you lots of ideas for lively patterns. Flowers, fish, birds and butterflies all offer a great deal of scope. When using animals or figures, do not try to copy them exactly. Instead, simplify the outline as much as possible. Then decorate them and try to make them fill the whole area you have allowed for them.

9

ABCDEFG
H ABCDEFG M
N HIJKLM S
TUVWXYZ

Lettering

Lettering on cards should be treated as a form of pattern making, whether it is used on its own or with other shapes or motifs. The message should never look as if it has been added as an afterthought. The lettering is as important to the design as the shape of the card itself.

Think of each letter as a shape which, when put with other similar shapes, makes up a more complicated pattern. These words or patterns can then be used with illustration to build up the final design. Neat handwriting combines with illustration quite well.

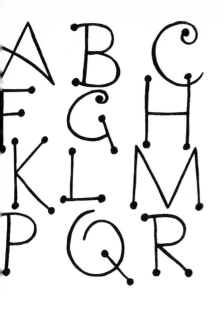

If the lettering is to be the only decoration on the card, the spaces between the letters become particularly important. Never measure the spaces between the letters to make them exactly equal. The more carefully you measure, the more *uneven* the spacing will appear.

Try cutting letters from magazines and shifting them about on the card until they look correct before pasting them down. Use the spaces as shapes in your pattern in the same way as you use the letters.

Look at the bottom alphabet on the left. It has become a pattern of light and dark shapes. The light shapes are a mixture of letters and spaces, and so are the dark ones.

Aries
the ram
(March 21–
April 19)

Taurus
the bull
(April 20–May 20)

Gemini
the twins
(May 21–June 20)

Cancer
the crab
(June 21–July 22)

Leo
the lion
(July 23–
August 22)

Virgo
the virgin
(August 23–
September 22)

Libra
the scales
(September 23–
October 22)

Scorpio
the scorpion
(October 23–
November 21)

Sagittarius
the archer
(November 22–
December 21)

Capricornus
the goat
(December 22–
January 19)

Aquarius
the water-carrier
(January 20–
February 18)

Pisces
the fishes
(February 19–
March 20)

12

Signs and symbols

All kinds of signs and symbols will provide excellent shapes for a design. Signs of the Zodiac (facing page) make particularly attractive cards. Choose the right sign and cut it out of coloured paper or pieces of dress fabric.

You could make a 'Good Luck' card in a similar way using a 'lucky' sweep, horeshoe or four-leaved clover.

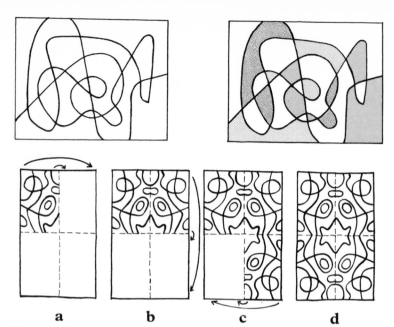

a   b   c   d

Repeating patterns
Taking a line for a walk

1 Allow your pencil to wander freely over a piece of paper, curving back and crossing itself at a number of points. Take it over the edges of the paper once or twice and then finish the line where you began it.

2 Trace the pattern. Turn the tracing face down and draw over the same lines.

3 Take a sheet of paper four times the size of the tracing. Fold it in half and in half again. Open it out and lay the tracing in the top left-hand section. Draw over the lines of the tracing, **a**.

4 Turn the tracing over from left to right and fit it in the top right-hand section. Draw over the lines again, **b**.

5 Turn the tracing over again, this time from top to bottom. Fit it in the bottom right-hand section of the paper and draw over the lines again, **c**.

6 Turn the tracing one last time, this time from right to left. Fit it into the final section and draw over the design once more, **d**.

You have now made a symmetrical repeating pattern ready for painting or colouring.

There are many other ways of making repeating patterns. Look how these designs link up and notice how the top one seems to change when the second row is placed differently.

Potato prints

It is easy to print all-over repeating patterns like those at the foot of page 15. All you need to make the printing block is a knife and a potato.

1 Cut the potato in half.

2 Test the cut surface by painting it and pressing it firmly onto a piece of newspaper. You may have to rock the potato slightly to and fro to make sure that all the edges come in contact with the paper.

3 If the print shows areas of white, the cut surface is uneven. Slice the potato again and try once more.

4 Trim the printing area to shape. (Rectangles are best as they join easily together.)

5 Mark the pattern onto the printing surface using V-shaped cuts. Do not cut away too much of the potato. You can always add more cuts later, but pieces cannot be replaced once they have been cut away.

6 Paint the cut surface and make some practice prints to see how thick the paint should be. Tempera blocks are ideal for potato prints, but other paints may be used instead. Try out prints on different kinds of paper and see how the results vary.

On the facing page are two quite different designs printed with the same potato block.

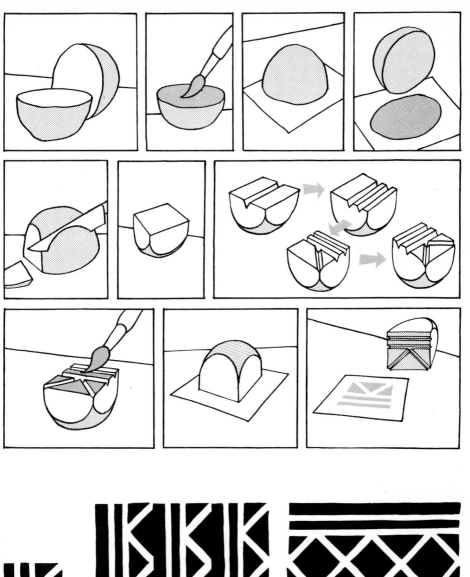

Leaf prints

Leaves make excellent printing surfaces and are much more suitable for informal arrangements than for making regular patterns. Arrange the prints so that they look like fallen or growing leaves. You can add a focal point by placing a larger, stronger, or more colourful print over the top of several weaker ones.

Paint one side of the leaf making sure that all the edges are well covered.

Lay the printed surface downwards on the paper.

Place a backing sheet of paper or thin cardboard over the leaf.

Press firmly with the fingertips, smoothing all over the leaf. Be very careful not to move the leaf or backing sheet as you do so. Make sure that the edges and centre vein of the leaf are well pressed.

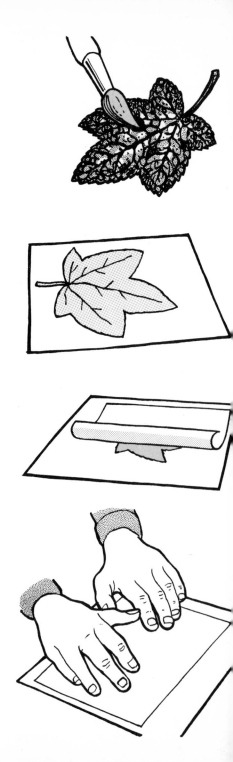

If, when looking for leaves to print with, you find a well-preserved leaf skeleton, you could glue it straight onto a card like the one on the left.

Notice the informal placing of the leaves in the prints below.

Collage

Very attractive and unusual cards may be made in collage using all kinds of natural and man-made materials.

Seeds

The two cards below use seeds of different colours, shapes and sizes. The smaller card was made by covering parts of the surface with paste and then shaking small seeds over it while still wet. The surplus seeds were removed when the paste had dried a little. The remaining areas were then pasted and contrasting seeds shaken onto them.

The larger card makes use of the wandering line described on page 14. The design was drawn onto the card and filled in with sunflower, iris and wheat seeds. Lighter-coloured melon seeds fill in the background.

Corrugated cardboard was used for the design on the left.

Lay two sheets of cardboard together with the ridges running at right angles to each other. Cut the pattern through both sheets and then fit the interlocking shapes together like a jigsaw.

Boxes of chocolates and candies are often packed with suitable coloured corrugated paper.

The lion design on the card below was made with spaghetti, macaroni, rice and peppercorns.

Found objects

Use a clear, quick-drying, multi-purpose adhesive to fix heavy materials such as nails and screws to your card. As their weight may cause the card to overbalance you may have to taper the back flap so that the card leans backwards. Make a pencil mark on the outer edge of the back flap about 1·5 cm (or ½ in.) from the bottom. Draw a straight line from that mark to the bottom of the centre fold and cut along the line.

Feathers are an interesting material for making a collage. Use just the tips and overlap them to hide the trimmed ends.

Seed catalogues

Cut out flowers to paste over the whole face of the card, working from the edges towards the centre.

Alternatively, you could cut a lace paper frill (diags. **a**, **b**, **c**) to make a card like the one on page 52.

When trimming flowers to fit your card, try re-shaping the petals **d**, or hide the straight edges with sections from other flowers, **e**.

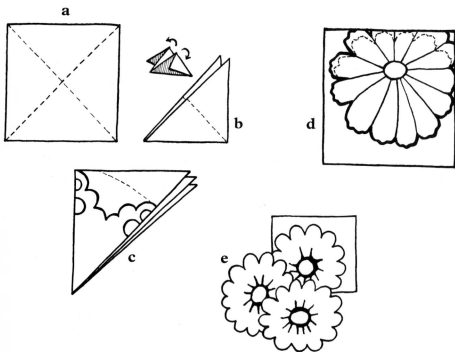

a

b

c

d

e

24

a   b   c

Pressed flowers

Collect flowers throughout the year – with stems on whenever possible – and arrange the petals carefully before pressing.

Arrange the flowers on the card in natural rhythms. (It may help to draw some guide-lines first, **a**.) Glue the smaller, outer flowers in position, **b**, and build the design inwards hiding the ends of stems with larger blooms. Finish with a larger, colourful bloom just off the centre, **c**.

Colour photograph page 52.

Folding and cutting

Simple folding

The simplest card to make is a decorated flat surface like a postcard. To make a card stand up, you have to fold it and we have grown accustomed to simple folded cards opening on the right.

A single fold will make a rigid card if the paper is stiff enough, but paper will normally have to be folded twice, **a**. The larger it is, the stiffer the paper or cardboard must be so that it will not flop or fall over with each gust of wind.

Folds will not only make a card stronger and help it stand more firmly, but they will also make it look more interesting. There is no need at all to fold cards in the traditional way. You could fold both sides of the card into the centre, **b**, or you could make alternating folds like a concertina, **c**. Diagonal folds will make a triangular card, **d**.

Flaps may be glued to the back or front of the card to make it stand more firmly or to add interest to the design.

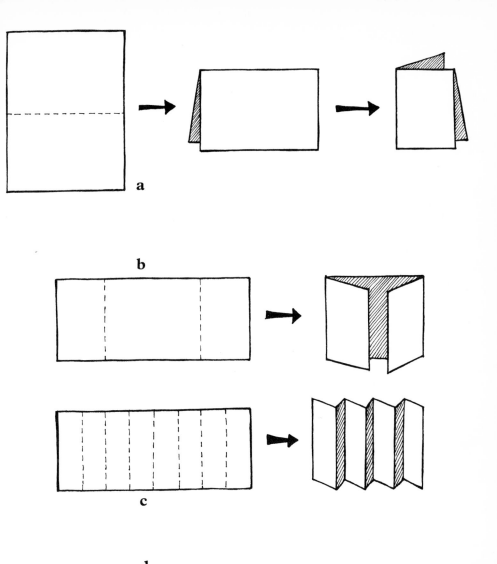

a

b

c

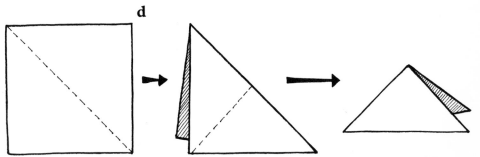

d

27

Folded flaps can be made to hide part of a design to make a surprise card.

For card **a**, divide the paper into three sections and fold the left-hand one into the centre.

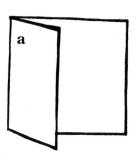

Card **c** is folded in the same way as card **b**. (You might like to write a message or the person's name in the twists in the flute.)

To make sure that the two halves fit, draw the design onto the closed card, then open it out and fill in the centre.

To make card **b** divide
the paper into three
equal sections. Fold
the left-hand section across
as for card **a**, and then fold
it back in half again. Do
the same with the right-
hand section.

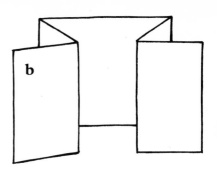

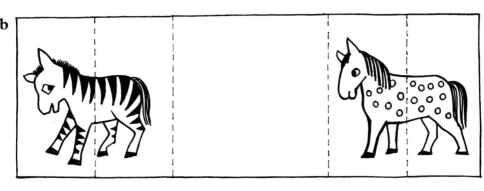

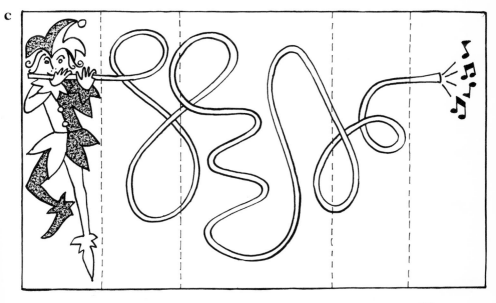

Doors and windows

You can hide a message behind a door or window cut in the front flap of a card.

To make card **a**, cut along the solid lines, through one thickness of the paper only, and fold the door back along the dotted line.

Card **b** has a double window. Cut along the solid lines, starting and finishing at the fold in the card.

For card **c**, fold the paper into a concertina, with each of the sections the same size, and open it out again. Cut five doors ranging down in size, as shown in the diagram. (Cut along solid lines, fold along dotted lines.) Fold up the concertina, spreading glue on the outer edges of the door frames as you do so. There will now be no less than five doors to open before the message can be read.

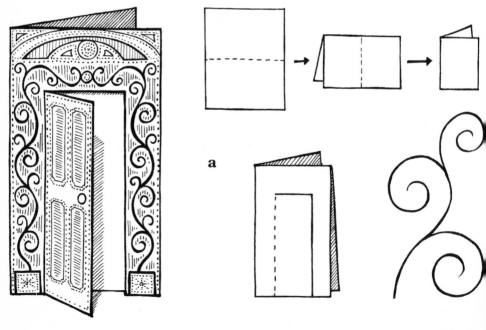

a

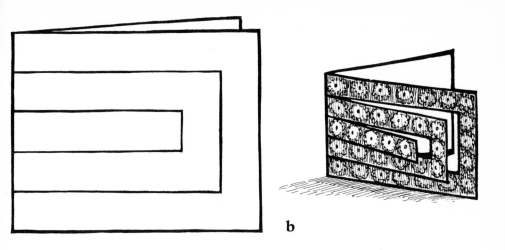

b

c

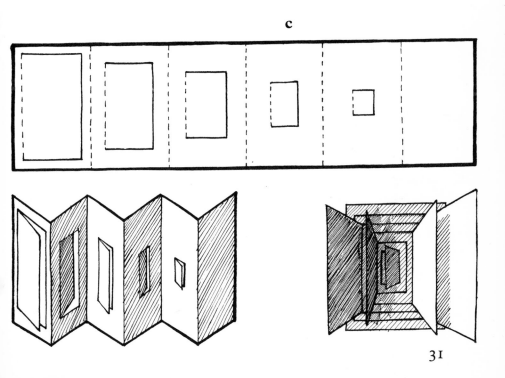

Coloured windows

Coloured cellophane paper will catch and hold or reflect the light in interesting ways.

To make the left-hand card on the facing page, cut out the front of the card leaving just a stiff frame round the edge. Paste clear cellophane to the back of the frame and then glue on a design of coloured cellophane or tissue paper shapes. Let some of the shapes overlap for subtle colour effects.

To make 'stained glass windows', draw a design in chalk or light-coloured pencil on black cardboard. Double the lines so that they look like railway tracks and then cut out the different shapes between them. The 'railway tracks' should be quite close together so that the strips of black cardboard that are left when the shapes have been cut out are narrow enough to resemble the leaded part of the window. Paste coloured cellophane over the holes. Candy wrappers are the ideal material for this.

These cards are most effective when stood on a window-sill so that the light shines through them.

Metal foil

Cards decorated with metal foil are also attractive on a windowsill (see photograph opposite). To make one, cut a lacy paper pattern as shown on page 24. Lay it on a sheet of kitchen foil and draw round it using an empty ball-point pen. Turn the foil over and draw round each side of this outline (dotted lines on diagram). Add a 'scribble' background to give texture, and mount the foil on a cardboard base.

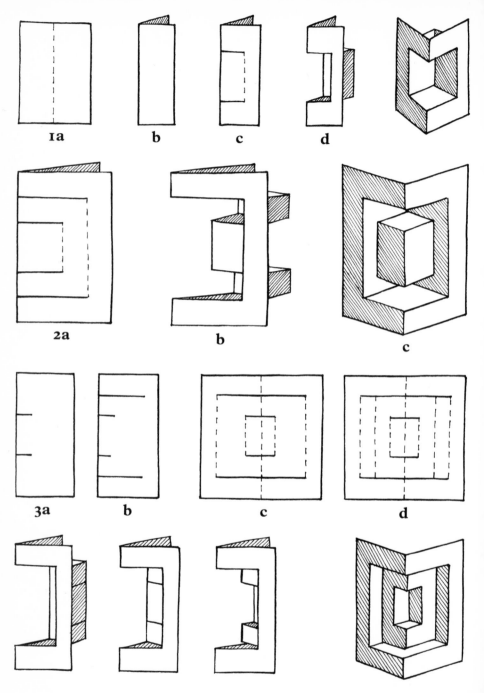

1a   b   c   d

2a   b   c

3a   b   c   d

Cutting and folding

Card 1 Fold a rectangle of stiff paper or thin cardboard in half, **b**. Make two straight cuts of equal length from the fold towards the edges, **c**. Crease the centre section inwards along the dotted lines, **d**.

Card 2 Make in the same way as for the first card, but with two pairs of cuts (solid lines, diagram **a**). The second pair should be shorter and should come inside the first ones. Crease the whole of the centre section inwards, **b**, as for card 1, then fold the small middle section back again, **c**.

Card 3 Cut the cardboard along the solid lines in diagrams **a** and **b** and fold along the dotted lines in diagrams **c** and **d**. Crease the whole of the centre section inwards along the outer dotted lines and then back again along the middle ones. Crease the small middle section inwards. (Photograph page 52, top right.)

Cards 4 and 5 Cut along the solid lines in the diagrams and crease sections inwards along dotted lines.

4   5

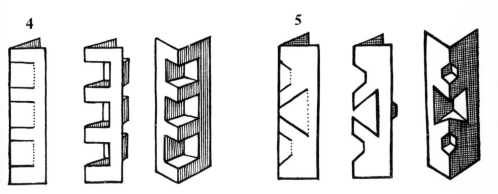

These two cards have been decorated with gummed paper shapes. You will find diagrams for folding them on pages 27 and 36. Try to cut all edges cleanly and press all folds and creases firmly, running your fingernail along them to make them extra sharp.

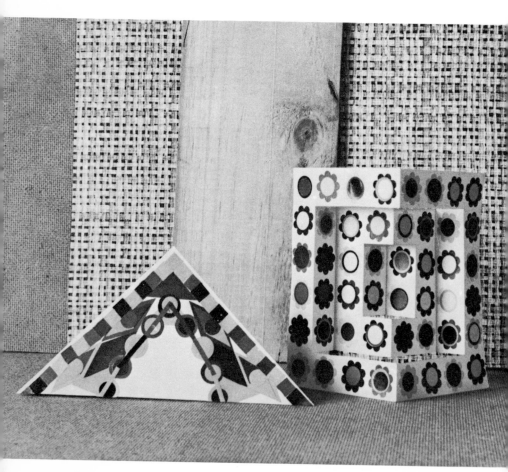

This hen and chick make use of the folding and cutting method described on pages 36 and 37.

Draw the bird shapes as shown in the diagram. Cut along the solid lines. Score along the dotted lines with the point of your scissors and fold them alternately down and up.

Decorate with lettering or feather patterns.

As well as being an attractive birthday card, this design would be very appropriate as a card for sending Easter greetings.

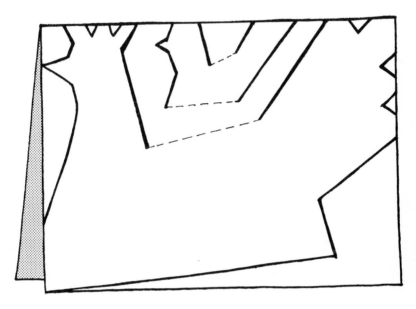

Animal cards

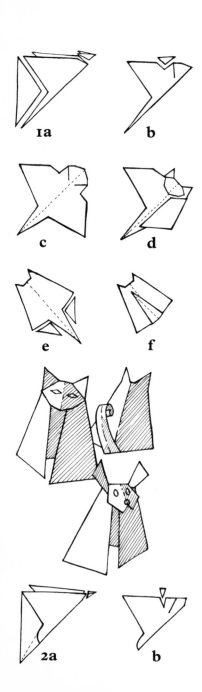

1a

b

c

d

e

f

2a

b

Cat
Start with a square of paper. Fold it diagonally in half.

Cut portions away to shape the tail and nose, **1a**.

Cut a notch and a slit to shape the head, **b**.

Open the paper out flat, **c**. Fold the side flaps in to the centre and bend the head forward, **d**.

Turn the cat face down, **e**. Trim off the ends of the flaps.

Bend up the tail, **f**, and curl it round a pencil.

Dog
Start off as for the cat, with a square of paper folded diagonally in half.

Use diagrams **2a** and **b** as guides for trimming the nose and tail.

Open out the paper and fold the sides in to the middle. Trim them across the bottom, **c**.

Fold down the head, **d**.

Basic shapes
These may be used for animals, faces and figures of your own invention.

c

d

Tube Fold a rectangle of paper in half so that the narrow edges are almost level but not quite, **1a**. Fold back the longer side into a flap, **b**. Stick the two halves together by spreading glue along the flap, **b**. To make a square-sided tube, open it out and fold it so that the two creases meet, **c**.

Cone Draw shape **2a** on a sheet of paper. Add a flap one side, **b**, and a slit the other. Roll it up and fit the slit into the flap, **c**.

Pyramid Follow diagrams **3a**, **b**, **c** and **d**. Cut along solid lines, fold along dotted ones. Fold the paper into a pyramid. Overlap the two outer sections and glue them together.

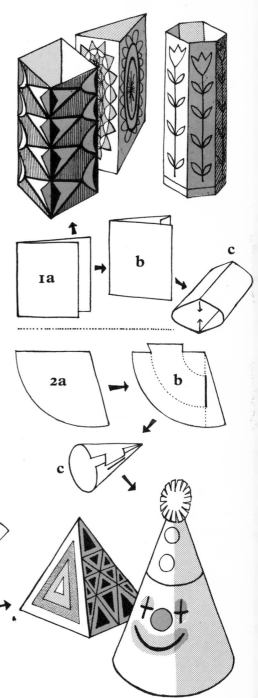

Instructions and diagrams for making this Christmas
reindeer appear on page 44 and the *hen and her chick*
are on page 39. The *cat* and *dog* are on page 40.

Using these basic folds and those on page 41 you can
invent other animal figures and faces of your own.

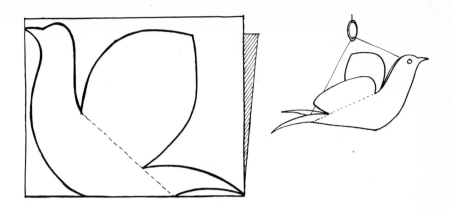

Flying bird

Draw the outline on a folded piece of paper as shown. Bend the wings down. Thread a curtain ring onto a piece of cotton and attach the ends to the head and tail of the bird so that it can be hung up.

Butterfly

Start as for the bird, diagram **a**. Cut out the butterfly. Fold the wings down along the dotted line nearest the insect's body, then fold them back up again along the other dotted line. To send the card through the post, open out the body but leave the wings folded, **b**.

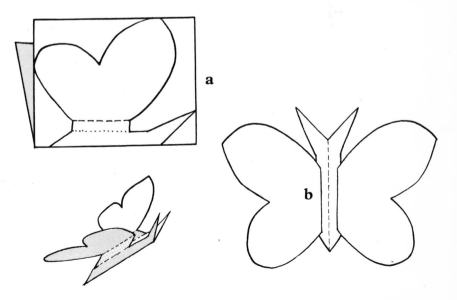

Snowman Make a round tube with two flaps and two slits. Paint your design while the card is flat or glue one onto the finished tube. Do not glue the flaps in position. The card must be sent flat through the post.

Santa Make a cone (instructions page 41). Glue on a beard and a pom-pom with just a dab of glue on the centre of each. They will then stand partly free when the cone is formed.

Tree There are two ways of making one of the Christmas tree cards shown opposite. They appear on page 46.

Reindeer This is made from a square tube as described on page 41. The shading round the reindeer marks the area to be cut away.

Cracker A card with an ordinary simple fold, turned on its side and trimmed to shape.

Try making Christmas cards using other folds or methods of decoration described in this book.

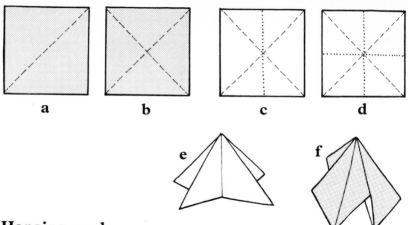

Hanging cards

(*Above*) Fold a square of paper along the lines shown
in diagrams **a** and **b**. Open out the paper after each
folding. Turn it over and add the extra folds shown
in **c** and **d**. The paper square will then make shape
e or, if turned inside out, shape **f**. Use **e** for the Christmas
tree on page 45.

(*Below*) You need four rectangles of paper the same
size for this hanging card. Fold them in half and draw
exactly the same design on each. (Draw only half of
the design, using the fold as an imaginary line down
the centre.) Glue the four pieces together, **c**, and trim
round the outlines, **d** and **e**. Attach a piece of cotton
to the top.

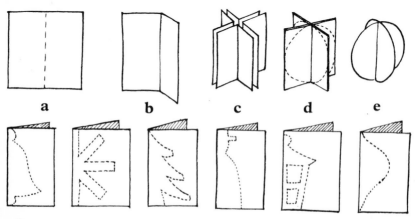

Novelty cards

Valentine cards
(*Top*) Make a bluebird or dove as described on page 43 to support a single folded card decorated with a heart.

(*Bottom*) Trim a single-fold card into a heart shape and glue lace round the edge. Support it on both sides with paper birds.

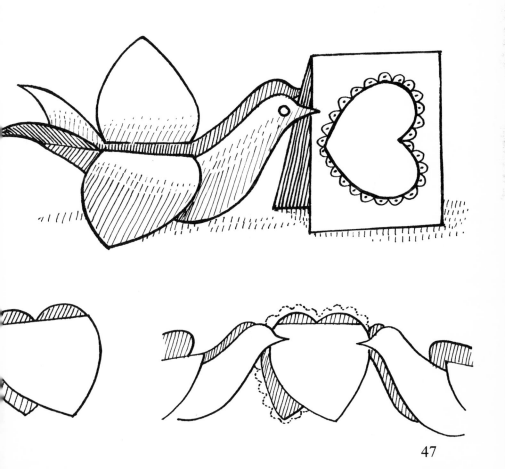

Padded cards

These can be made quite simply using sheets of plastic foam as padding.

First prepare a background of stiff cardboard covered with plain fabric. Cut out a heart – or whatever shape you have chosen for your design – in patterned fabric. (Make a paper pattern to cut round.) Cut a smaller heart in plastic foam and then an even smaller one. Lay the hearts on top of each other on the cardboard, the smallest one underneath and the fabric one on top. Tuck the edge of the fabric round the edge of the foam and glue it to the background with quick-drying glue. Decorate it with lace or other trimmings.

Revolving cards

Revolving cards may be used to spell out a message, a name, or show a changing scene. The instructions are ideal for a New Year's card as the disc is divided into twelve sections, but other divisions would allow a short message or name to be spelt out.

Draw a large circle on white cardboard and cut it out. Draw a small circle in the centre and a larger one just inside the circumference (diagram **g**, page 50). Make a second cardboard circle exactly the same.

Divide one of the cardboard circles into four by drawing two straight lines through the centre, **a**. Set your compasses to the same radius as the very first circle you drew. With the point on **x** and then on **y** make marks on the circumference as shown in **a**, **b** and **c**. Draw straight lines from all these points across

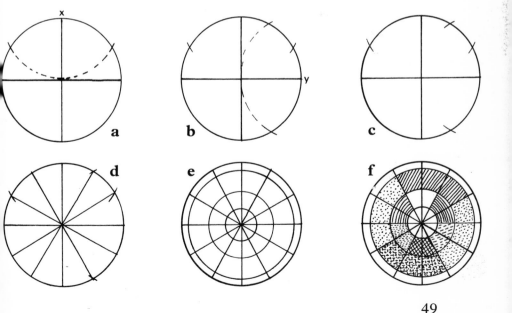

to the opposite side of the circle, **d**. The cardboard circle is now divided into twelve sections, one for each month. If you wish, you can divide each month into 'earth' and 'sky'. The card will now look like diagram **e**. Colour in a different design or symbol for each month.

Measure the width of the top and the bottom of one of the months. Draw a window with these measurements on your second cardboard circle and cut it out, **h**. Make a hole through the centre of both cardboard circles and join them with a paper clip.

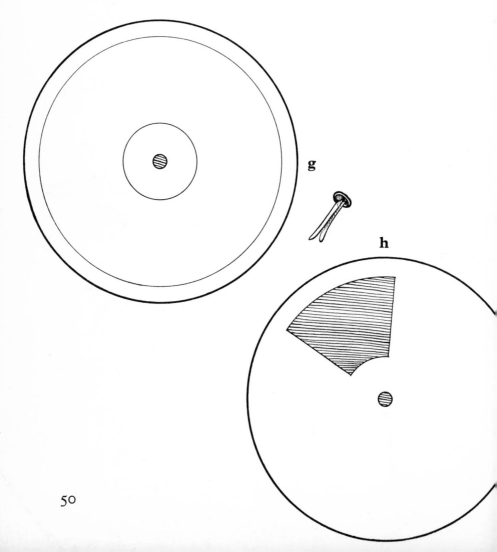

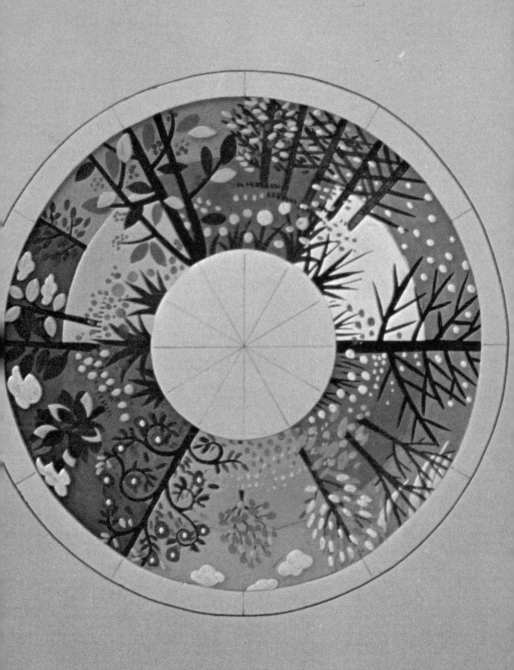

Puzzle messages

If you have a friend who loves solving puzzles, why not send him a card with a distorted message.

Draw the letters as tall and thin and close together as you possibly can, like the ones on this page. Make the horizontal strokes thicker than they would normally be.

To read the message your friend will have to hold the card level with his eyes so as to look along the letters.

Opposite
Instructions for making the cat, the triangular card and the folded card are in pages 40, 26 and 37 respectively.

These single-fold cards with collage decoration are described on pages 24 and 25.

Pop-up cards

Make an ordinary single fold card. Decide on your design – it might be a fort like this one, or a garden with bushes and rose-covered arches, or even a Christmas scene.

Paint the background onto the card. Fold some strips of stiff paper as in diagram **a** and glue them onto the card, **b**. They can all be different heights and lengths, but the shaded parts must be exactly parallel with the back of the card.

Now cut out your trees, figures or buildings and glue them onto the fronts of the strips, **c**. None of these shapes should overlap the edges of the card when it is closed.

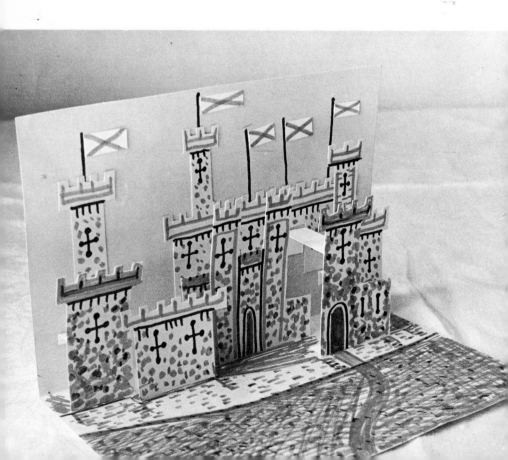

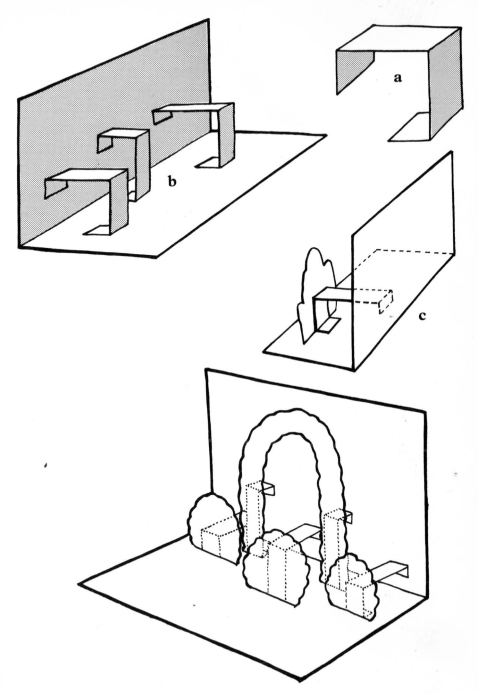

Jack-in-the-box

Make a single fold card. Draw the outline of the figure on stiff paper, **a**. Cut it out and crease it along the dotted lines, **b**. (The easiest way to do this is to leave the figure folded in half when making the creases. Then, with the figure half opened out, and holding the body section, push the legs forward and up, the arms forward and down, and the head further forward and down.)

Paint or colour the figure and glue the body section only into the fold in the card. Cut and fold a strip of stiff paper for the 'box', **d**, decorate it and glue it in position.

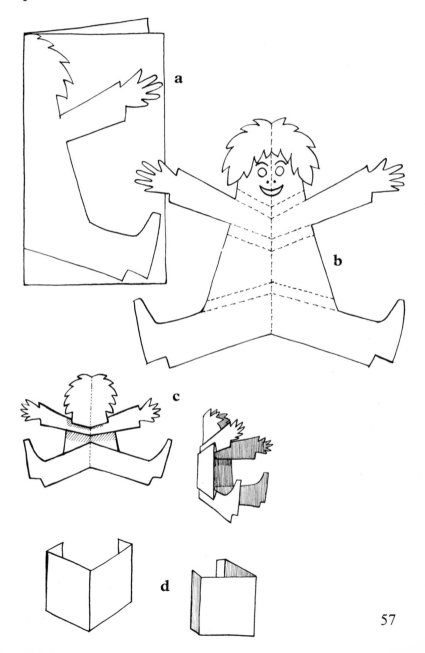

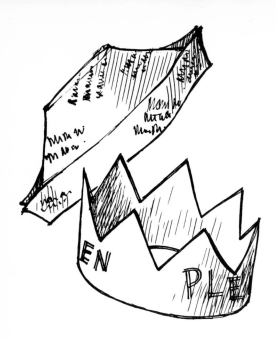

Party invitations

These are not cards at all, really, but they are fun to make. Write the invitations with felt pen on paper hats made out of newspaper, or on inflated balloons. (You will have to let the balloons down to send them through the post, of course.)

Rattles

A baby brother or sister would probably like a card that rattles. Paint a rattle on the front. Put some beads or rice in a tiny box and *glue the lid on firmly*. Glue the box inside the card.

Mobiles

A baby likes watching things that move. Make a snake or windmill card (opposite) or one of those described on page 46.

Stitched cards

Stitched designs make unusual greetings cards and, although they look complicated, are simple to make. You need thin cardboard, a darning needle, and wool, embroidery silk or thin string. The design on the facing page is built up of four squares, with design **c** stitched in opposite corners of each square.

Draw two sides of a square. Pierce holes at regular distances along them, **a**. (A large darning needle is ideal for this.)

Thread your needle and tie a large knot in the end of the wool or string. Bring the needle up through hole 1.

Push the needle down through hole 2 and up through 3, down through 4 and up through 5, down through 6 and up through 7.

Continue working towards the corner along one side of the square and away from it along the other until design **c** is complete.

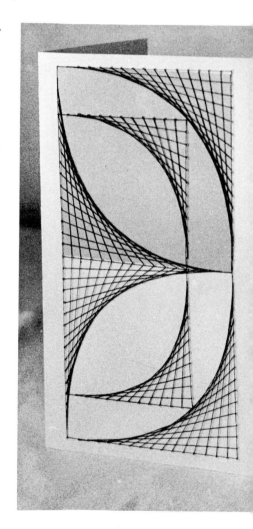

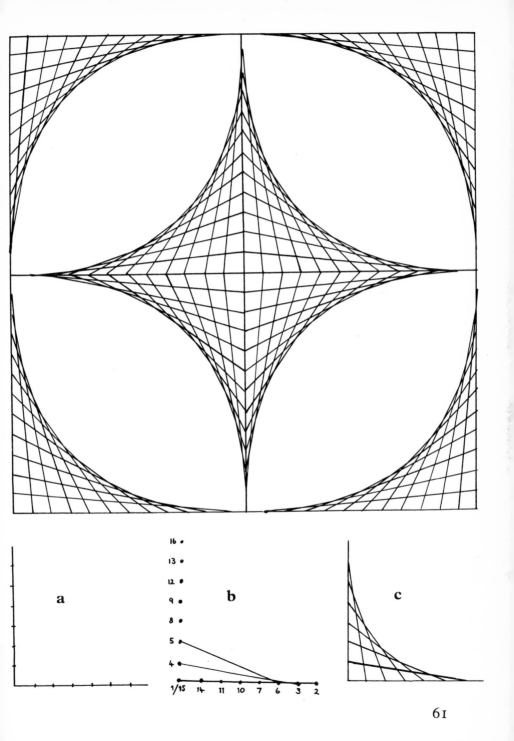

a

16 •
13 •
12 •
9 •
8 •
5 •
4 •

b

1/15 14 11 10 7 6 3 2

c

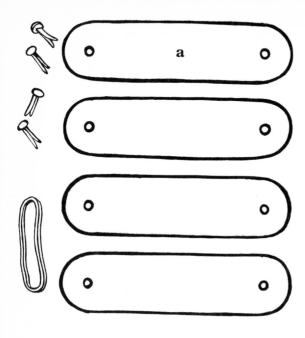

Snappers

These are two cards for practical jokers.

'*Jumper*' Cut four identical pieces of strong cardboard and make a hole at each end, **a.** Join them into a square with paper clips. Make sure the joints move easily.

Loop a small elastic band over the paper clips on opposite corners (diagram **b**). Push the other two corners together stretching the elastic band (diagram **c**).

Put the 'Jumper' into a narrow envelope. The envelope must hold the two sides together that keep the elastic band stretched. You may have to make your own envelope so as to have a perfect fit.

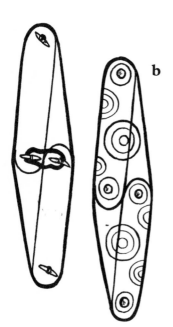

b

c

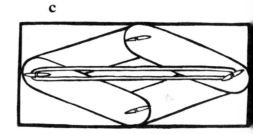

'*Mousetrap*' Cut out two stiff paper hinges and two pieces of stiff cardboard using diagram **d** as a guide. (The smaller piece of cardboard is exactly the same width but only half as long as the larger piece.)

d

e

f

Cut a notch in one of the narrow ends of the larger piece of cardboard. It should be wide enough for the elastic band and should reach to the centre of the card.

Fix the smaller piece of cardboard to the centre of the larger one using the stiff paper hinges. Bend this card flap down away from the notch and slip the elastic band down the notch and over the two thicknesses of cardboard (diagram **e**).

To 'set the trap' fold the card flap over against the notched end of the base, **f**. This will stretch the elastic band. Write a suitable message on the back and then slip the mousetrap inside a stiff envelope.

Angler
This is an ideal card to send to anyone who enjoys fishing. As the card is opened the angler seems to wind in his fish.

Make a single fold card and draw or paint the angler sitting on a bank and holding his rod on the front. Make a hole at the end of the rod right through both thicknesses of card.

Tie a knot in the end of a piece of thin string and thread it through from the back of the card. Tie a card or paper fish on the end.

A 'woven' fish makes an unusual species for the angler to catch. Instructions are given on page 66.

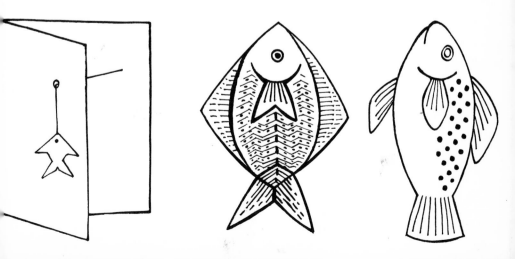

Woven fish

Weave your fish from two long thin strips of paper. (You may find the diagrams easier to follow if you use two different colours.)

Do not crease the strips until the fish shape is complete. Pull the fin and tail pieces gently to make it firm.

Follow the diagrams for step by step instructions. After step **d**, turn the fish over to produce diagram **e**. When you reach step **g**, pull the strips firm and press them flat. Trim off the tail and fins at an angle.

Your fish is now ready to attach to the angler's line (page 65).

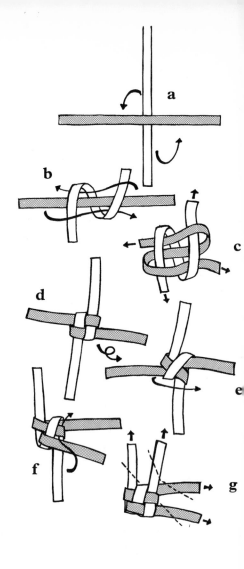

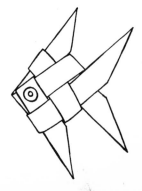

Which card for which occasion?

Most of the cards in this book can be adapted to fit any occasion, but here are some ideas to start you off.

All fools day (April 1) snappers 62
Birthday, babies and toddlers: hanging cards 46, jack-in-the-box 56, rattles and mobiles 58–59
    fathers and brothers: angler 64, fort 54, nail collage 22
    general: decorative lettering 10, leaf prints for autumn birthdays 18, pressed flowers for summer birthdays 25, repeating patterns 14, zodiac cards 12–13
    grandfathers and uncles: garden pop-up 55, puzzle cards 53
    grandmothers and aunts: collage 20, stitched cards 60–61
    mothers and sisters; flower cards 24, potato prints 16, signs of the Zodiac 12
Christmas (December 25) cracker 44, hanging cards 46, metal foil 35, pop-ups 54, reindeer 44, Santa 44, snowman 44, tree 44, 46
Easter feathered card 23, hen and chick 39
Good Luck cat 40, lucky sweep 13
New Year (January 1) doors 30, revolving cards 49–51
St Valentine's Day (February 14) hanging bird 43, padded cards 48, Valentine cards 47

Index